BOA
EDITIONS LTD

LIGHT AND HEAVY THINGS

LIGHT AND HEAVY THINGS

Selected Poems of
Zeeshan Sahil

Translated from the Urdu by
Faisal Siddiqui, Christopher Kennedy,
and Mi Ditmar

BOA Editions, Ltd. ～ Rochester, NY ～ 2013

First Edition
13 14 15 16   7 6 5 4 3 2 1

For information about permission to reuse any material from this book, please contact The Permissions Company at www.permissionscompany.com or e-mail permdude@eclipse.net.

Publications by BOA Editions, Ltd.—a not-for-profit corporation under section 501 (c) (3) of the United States Internal Revenue Code—are made possible with funds from a variety of sources, including public funds from the New York State Council on the Arts, a state agency; the Literature Program of the National Endowment for the Arts; the County of Monroe, NY; the Lannan Foundation for support of the Lannan Translations Selection Series; the Mary S. Mulligan Charitable Trust; the Rochester Area Community Foundation; the Arts & Cultural Council for Greater Rochester; the Steeple-Jack Fund; the Ames-Amzalak Memorial Trust in memory of Henry Ames, Semon Amzalak and Dan Amzalak; and contributions from many individuals nationwide.

Cover Design: Daphne Morrissey
Cover Photo: Jay Muhlin
Interior Design and Composition: Richard Foerster
Manufacturing: McNaughton & Gunn
BOA Logo: Mirko

Library of Congress Cataloging-in-Publication Data

Sahil, Zeeshan, 1961–2008.
[Poems. Selections]
Light and heavy things: the selected poems of Zeeshan Sahil / translated by Faisal Siddiqui, Christopher Kennedy, and Mi Ditmar.
    pages cm. — (Lannan Translations Selection Series)
Poems.
ISBN 978-1-938160-12-7 (Paper) — ISBN 978-1-938160-13-4 (E-Book)
I. Title.
PR9540.9.S24L5413 2013
821'.92—dc23
                        2012044348

Lannan

BOA Editions, Ltd.
250 North Goodman Street, Suite 306
Rochester, NY 14607
www.boaeditions.org
A. Poulin, Jr., Founder (1938–1996)

This book is dedicated to the memory of Zeeshan Sahil
(1961–2008)

Contents

⌒⌒

Foreword

In her biographical statement about Zeeshan Sahil in *Pakistani Urdu Verse: An Anthology*, which she translated and edited, Yasmeen Hameed, Writer in Residence at Lahore University of Management Science (LUMS), states that Sahil "sensitively transforms the mundane and trivial into a highly reflective and moving poetic expression." Sahil, who passed away in 2008, was among a small group of Pakistani poets, including Javed Shaheen, Afzal Ahmed Syed, and Nasreen Anjum Bhatti, who wrote prose poems, which, in this case, means poems unfettered by conventional uses of meter and rhyme. Though perhaps not exactly what comes to mind for readers of contemporary American poetry (Sahil's prose poems are more like free verse), the poems lend themselves to translation more readily than the ghazal, a form of Urdu poetry more familiar to readers of Pakistani poetry in translation.

Sahil was born in Hyderabad, Sindh, in 1961 and died in Karachi in 2008. He published eight collections of poetry in Urdu: *Arena* (1985), *Chirion ka Shor* (1989), *Kuhr Alood Aasmaan kay Sitaaray* (1994), *Karachi aur Doosri Nazmein* (1995), *Email aur Doosri Nazmein* (2003), *Shabnama aur Doosri Nazmein* (2003), *Jang ke Dinon Mein* (2003) and *Neem-tareek Muhabbat* (2005). The poems in this collection were culled from all of the books with the exception of the first, *Arena*, in an attempt to provide an overview of the poet's evolution over the course of his writing life.

I was introduced to the work of Zeeshan Sahil by my student, Raza Ali Hasan, in 2005. Ali approached me about an independent study, which would consist of his doing literal translations of some Pakistani poets writing in Urdu, and my revising the literal drafts into functional poems in English. My knowledge of Urdu was and still is nonexistent, and the only Pakistani poet whose poems I knew fairly well was Faiz Ahmed Faiz, whose work was translated by my friend and wonderful poet, the late Agha Shahid Ali. After attempting to translate Faiz we began work on Sahil's poems. I was immediately intrigued, especially by the first of the translations, "Black Bird," the poem that begins this collection, a decidedly postmodern poem that contained images I could not shake. In particular:

> The cage was empty,
> and the vase in your window
> overflowed with white flowers.

And also:

> I stared out the window.
> Dreams built their nests in my eyes,
> and the cage was empty.

Over the next few months, we translated several of Sahil's poems, publishing some of them in *The Annual of Urdu Studies*, and, encouraged by the editor there, Dr. Muhammad Umar Memon, we continued. Eventually, my wife, Mi Ditmar, began working with us. Having grown up in a bilingual family (her mother is Latvian) she was able to help with the nuances of syntax, and she often had insights about some of the more abstract aspects of the poems that gave the finished products a more concrete and Western-friendly tone. Again, we published some of the poems in *The Annual*, and we began to think in terms of a collection of Sahil's poems. Through Dr. Memon, I contacted Sahil, and he sent me his books, which arrived sewn between two pieces of faded white cloth, along with a handwritten note from Mr. Sahil, expressing his thanks for our interest in his work, and a piece of paper that indicated the contents of the package had been inspected by someone in the Pakistan government. Not long after I received the books, Mr. Sahil passed away at the age of forty-seven. He had been confined to a wheelchair due to a birth deformity and had struggled with health problems his entire life.

By now, Ali had moved on to other projects, and he recommended a poet friend from Pakistan, now living in San Francisco, Faisal Siddiqui. Faisal was enthusiastic about the book, and he took over the role of doing the literal translations. He had met Sahil in Karachi a few times, and his father knew him as well.

Faisal began sending us his literal translations, and he helped us revise the earlier poems we had done with Ali. Eventually, we published some of these in *The Annual*. Encouraged by the success we had with the poems, we decided to put together a manuscript. After accumulating a book's worth of poems, some of the predominant features of Sahil's work become apparent. There are simple images of the natural world, often in conflict with the world human beings have made, either literal walls ("Wall and Bird") or barriers of the mind ("East"), as well as images of war, where a swarm of bicycles can stop a tank ("A Child's Bicycle"). There is an innocence in these poems combined with a worldliness that makes them disarming. They attend to the harsh realities of post-Cold War Pakistan, while offering an obstinate hopefulness, regardless of the outcome of the effort:

> The bird awakens
> and begins breaking down the wall
> from morning to night,
> keeps breaking it down
> from night to morning.
>
> One morning the wall notices
> the bird has broken down.

That stubbornness of will exemplified by the bird (and birds appear often in Sahil's work, generic and symbolic flocks of them) serves as an excellent metaphor for his own tenacity. In an interview with Sahil on the website Dawn.com, he says, "If I did not write poetry then I would not have done anything. Writing poetry is my vocation and not a hobby or habit..."

At times deeply personal and at others overtly political, and, more often than not, a compelling hybrid of the two, the poems are simple and straightforward, subtle and strange. Their power is often hidden until the last image of the poem appears. In the beginning of "Birds," the speaker describes Karachi by refuting the lies that have been told about the city: "It is a lie / that after the rain in Karachi / the sprouting grass / doesn't have blades / deep green and soft." He continues by cataloging some truths about Karachi: "In Karachi, / birds that fly from trees / live with us / through the sound of bullets and bombs" and "Our books don't wait / inside cupboards for termites." He concludes with "and our hands / tear down the walls / that once buried us alive." In typical Sahil fashion, he depicts what is troubling about the city he loves (bullets and bombs; walls that once buried us alive) along with what makes the city appealing (blades deep green and soft; [o]ur books don't wait), culminating with the image of the citizenry digging themselves out from the rubble that once entombed them.

In the title poem, Sahil contrasts a shooting victim's "nearly weightless tears" with the "heavy gun" of the boy who shot him. The speaker imagines that if the tears were to fall on the gun, "one day the gun would rust, / or the boy's heart would go soft as wax." Here, as in "Wall and Bird," the organic (tears) confronts the man-made (heavy gun). However, the result is different. Instead of the man-made triumphing as when the bird collapses after trying to break down the wall, the gun becomes useless, and the shooter's heart melts. Of course, this is wishful thinking, but it speaks to the notion of hope that permeates the poems, despite their unflinching take on the atrocities of war and civil unrest.

In "Knife," the two extremes of the personal and political come together in an understated yet ultimately moving way. The speaker in "Knife" states, "From my loneliness, / a lantern takes shape / to be used in an emergency / during rainstorms." Light emerges from the darkness of his loneliness to provide a way of seeing in spite of the inclement weather. There is a sense of hopefulness out of despair, but also a sense of danger inherent in the emergency. The metaphor continues as the speaker explains that out of his loneliness a "carriage is made / to be used at tourist spots," a "bridge will be built / to be used during and after / the war for tanks to cross," and a "knife is honed / to cut paper or peel an apple." But the carriage may be needed when "the express train / derails" and the bridge may "suddenly be blown up."

And, most poignantly, when the knife "rusts, / it will be plunged into my heart." No longer useful as a pragmatic implement that cuts and peels, the knife becomes a means for the speaker to kill himself (or be murdered?). The matter-of-fact tone of the poem belies the ultimate shock of the ending. There are hints of destruction throughout, but the final image of suicide or murder is unexpected and invites a rereading of the earlier parts of the poem. The refrain of "From my loneliness" takes on a seriousness that could be overlooked on a first reading, and the images of the emergency, of derailment, of tanks crossing a bridge, become more than a backdrop for the speaker's sense of despair and more likely the reasons for it.

In "A Poem for You," the speaker states: "The world is the wrong place to live / if one has to live forever." The notion that the longer one exists the more difficult it would be to endure what the world has to offer might seem bleak, but Sahil undercuts the speaker's grim proclamation with a series of images that redeem the harshness: "But the happiness of riding on the bus / with Saiduddin, / and the melting wax from the candle burning / on your dressing table, / and the smoke collecting on your mirror / make up for everything." As with all of Sahil's poems, there is also a simply stated yet complex merging of the discomfort of living and its attendant beauty: "And in the city with all the blank street signs / when the night becomes darker, / your uneasy presence makes / the stars unnecessary, the moon redundant, / and the sea superfluous." The person to whom the speaker addresses this statement is "uneasy," yet her presence renders the natural world unnecessary. This negation implies that the most clichéd notions of poetic beauty are insignificant when compared to her. As usual, there is an uneasiness in the poem that mirrors the uneasiness in the beloved. The world is unendurable if one imagines oneself damned to never being able to leave it, but one individual's presence can render that notion irrelevant.

In many ways, Zeeshan Sahil remains a mystery to me. His poems as I know them, through the process of rendering the literal into the poetic, are as contemporary as any being written today in the United States, yet they come to me from a language that is much older than my own. Working with Faisal and Mi, I felt a bit like the speaker in "Poem," who says, "Whenever I travel / in the dark / I hide my face / with my hands / so the darkness / can't snatch it / away from me." I constantly had to ask myself and my co-translators, How do I do justice to the poems without putting my own face on them? I was working in the dark, relying on Faisal for the first drafts and on Mi for the fine-tuning that the poems so obviously needed. My own role seems dim to me now. I hope in some small way I contributed to creating what I believe is an important book by an important poet. It is my good fortune to have been given the opportunity to work on these poems and to have worked on them with such astute and intelligent co-translators. It is all of our good fortune that Sahil decided to write poetry, to follow his vocation. His poems are a gift; one that I hope still speaks as powerfully in English as they do in Urdu.

—Christopher Kennedy

LIGHT AND HEAVY THINGS

Black Bird

The cage was empty,
and the vase in your window
overflowed with white flowers.
In the bookstore, a new book
of poems had arrived.
The train in the station
waited to go: somewhere.
The cage was empty.
The black bird
flew a little ahead of the train.
Moving out of the tunnel,
the engine let out a scream.
I stared out the window.
Dreams built their nests in my eyes,
and the cage was empty.

A Poem for You

The world is the wrong place to live
if one has to live forever.
Each day life
would become more unbearable.
But the happiness of riding on the bus
with Saiduddin,
and the melting wax from the candle burning
on your dressing table,
and the smoke collecting on your mirror
make up for everything.
The flowers pressed in my book
grow into jungle dreams.
Your fingers trace many different paths
in the dust on the Formica.
And in the city with all the blank street signs
when the night becomes darker,
your uneasy presence makes
the stars unnecessary, the moon redundant,
and the sea superfluous.
Your memory and the mounting pressure
around my heart make me pray.
Despite the eternal anger of God toward poets,
my prayer always begins with you.

Poem

Be afraid of poets
They have hand grenade dreams
Let your words slip
And they'll throw them against the wall
Try to snatch them back
And they'll hide them under water
Whatever they have
They won't give you
If a mob confronts them
Even then the sky is theirs
They will call up a cavalry of clouds
And they will drown you
They own the earth and keep your footprints captive
They have a boat
And they'll ship you off
To an island and leave you there
If you live with birds you will forget
Faces of poets, your own face
When they come for you
You might push the birds in front of you
To take your place.

My Uncle's House

My sister goes to school.
My brother goes to work
or goes to meet his friends.

My uncle never goes anywhere;
he stays in his house. A house
all spring flowers and lush trees,
where the grass grows next to the wall
and having never seen the stars
dries up and grows taller.

This is where nothing is heard from the window.
This is where no one waves from the window.
This is where the door never opens for anyone.
When the birds start to squawk
no one minds or tries to silence them.
Even my uncle doesn't try to stop them.

He doesn't say a word.
Maybe he's angry with everyone,
with the birds, with me as well.

He doesn't speak to anyone.
He doesn't leave his house.
If someone calls, he doesn't answer.
I don't visit anymore.
It seems as if my uncle lives somewhere else,
far away from me.
And not in his house.

Taliban

Women will stay inside their homes
and girls will hide themselves;
flowers will blossom and wilt
on their branches.
A fog will obscure
the moon, the sun and the stars.
Birds in flight
will forget their songs,
and those that remain
in their nests
will die of fear.
They will dream a dream
of a life that is like a dream,
but when morning spreads its light
people will switch on their radios,
and the Taliban
will creep in through the window.

Birds

It is a lie
that after the rain in Karachi
the sprouting grass
doesn't have blades
deep green and soft.
Or that the trees
don't give shade
without the help of clouds.

And it's a lie
that our rabbits' eyes
don't shine in the dark
and squirrels
don't play with walnut shells.

Or that herbs
in the palm of the hand
yellow.
Snakes leave their share of milk
for the paper pythons.

In Karachi,
birds that fly from trees
live with us
through the sound of bullets and bombs;
perch on walls; always
they gather somewhere
to pray.

Our books don't wait
inside cupboards for termites.

Now our hearts
swim these seas
where once our eyes
searched for golden flowers
and our hands
tear down the walls
that once buried us alive.

What Does Suu Kyi Want?

Slender Suu Kyi
in her house in Rangoon:
What does she want?
Why won't she stop
the people from gathering outside her door
each day? She climbs the wooden stairs,
and from behind iron bars
she looks at them and wonders
at the brightness in their eyes…
All their impatient hearts are stilled.
Why won't Suu Kyi stop this
carnival? Outside her house, they tremble
and wait. Why won't she help them?
Outside her house soldiers display their guns,
passing by in lorries.
Why doesn't Suu Kyi fear them?
Why does tucking a flower behind her ear
like an ordinary housewife
make her so happy?
Why doesn't the fate of her people
bring Suu Kyi to tears?

Each day, why do the faces of tired citizens
make her smile?
Won't someone tell her to stop smiling?
Or snatch the flowers from her hair?
Time has made Suu Kyi fearless and strong.
Each day she becomes more fearless, more strong.
Perhaps now no one can look her in the eye.
Perhaps no one can even ask her:
What does she want?

I Will Send a Bird

I will send a bird
with shining wings.
It will come to you,
hidden in the clouds.
Maybe it will be evening
when it sees you drinking your tea.
The bird will laugh and laugh
when it sees you talking to the stars.
But you won't hear the laughter.
The bird will be tired, having traveled
so far a distance.
But you won't see.
The TV in your room will drone
while you fall asleep in front of it on the couch.
And above you in the skylight:
the bird with shining wings.
The bird I have sent.

Love

That girl I love who doesn't want
to read a poem begins a story—
A story so dark that no one can walk in it.
Love, usually found in such stories,
is absent.

Side by side, she walks with her favorite character.
But before she can reach the door
she stumbles.
She grasps the walls,
trying to stand up, and injures her fingers.
She cries when she finds
her beautiful nails are broken.

The story is still so dark
that no one can see her tears.

This girl is not the girl who began the story.
The girl who began the story is not the girl.

To move the story along,
she stumbles through the poem she had not read.

Step by step she gets to the end of her story.
She stays in the dark and travels far.
She moves through the dark and leaves love in the shadow
so that she can finish her story.

Knife

From my loneliness,
a lantern takes shape
to be used in an emergency
during rainstorms.
Or donated
to miners working in a gold mine.

From my loneliness,
a carriage is made
to be used at tourist spots.
Or when the express train
derails in bad weather.

From my loneliness,
a bridge will be built
to be used during and after
the war for tanks to cross.
Or to suddenly be blown up.

From my loneliness,
a knife is honed
to cut paper or peel an apple.
And when it rusts,
it will be plunged into my heart.

Poem

Get out of the house.
Go to the worn wooden bench
at the edge of the park.
Watch the sunlight vanish into dusk.
Far from you, on the dirt road,
the bells ring, the dust blows.
At the river's banks the boats arrive.
There are people on the boats.
There is joy in their faces
but not in your twilight.
They are far away from your life.
The bench at the end of the park
and the bench in your house
span the river's reach
or the length of the paved road your dreams walk.
For a while now there's been
no ringing of bells on the dirt road,
no boats at the riverbank,
no joy wrapped in dust.
Morning, the day: vanished; evening arrives,
the night comes on and yet, you never went to the park.
Not once.

Poetry

In these days of war
poetry
is a soldier's lover
or a bird's nest.
Nothing makes sense.
The sea is thrown into turmoil
from staring at the moon.
Sometimes a shell comes in
through the window of a house.
Nothing makes sense.
Suddenly disappearing
gossamer angels
and Saddam Hussein.
Nothing makes sense.
Except for the light that appears in the sky,
poetry leaves no trace of itself.
Except for tears in a girl's eye,
poetry can't be found.
It is an empty house,
its doors and windows stolen,
but the roof remains to shelter us from rain.
Or a tent
that can be burnt only by love
or a bridge that can't be reduced to splinters
by a tank or fighter plane.
Or a good Samaritan who takes
all the world's injured
in his arms and runs towards the infirmary.

Sun Stroke

Today the sun
rose in the west
and tried all day
to go east.
The dew on the trees
shone through the afternoon.
Today the grasshoppers
sang in remembrance of rain.
Birds sought their way
on the Siberian wind.
Today the sun, like a flower,
turned toward the moon
and by evening the moon
finished orbiting the earth.
Today people hung
the front doors of their houses
and set their mirrors
in the water
to catch the silver fish.

Time Bomb

I have a picture
and a wall that holds
the picture true.
And a nail that pierces
the picture and the wall
and punctures my breast.
I have a mirror and a candle
whose flame collects in the mirror.
And a cup that can't collect
rainwater or honey or wax.
I have a song that can be sung in the dark.
I have a story
that can only be told in the light.
I have a dream that can't be told to anyone.
I have a heart and nearby a time bomb
which is always ticking.

To Forget

Where were we going
before leaving each other?

Maybe I moved north to south
while you moved west to east.

Our faces turned away from each other,
and our hearts
were like vines that grow behind a wall,
putting down roots far away from it.
And you thoughtlessly
busy, trying to increase, a bit more,
the distance between us.
Not looking in any direction,
you moved away from me.

Poem

Whenever I travel
in the dark
I hide my face
with my hands
so the darkness
can't snatch it
away from me.

The Unworthy

The ones who think a flower
is a flower
and a star is a star
never go to the beach
on Sundays.
Never take the flowers,
given to them
on New Year's Eve,
out of their cellophane graves.

No new season
begins with their tears.
At spring's end
they dream no new dreams.
On rainy days they go to sleep
after closing the windows.
Or coming home from work
they step in the puddle
that hides the downed wire,
and they die
like those people
no one knows.

Untitled

This heart is a bomb
about to detonate.
But a martyr can't trigger it.
These eyes are bullets
engineered to go through the walls
and these hands, to stop
the onslaught of enemy tanks.
We have planted our feet on the ground.
(Everyone knows).

In the lull between wars,
we bought shoes for our children
and lanterns for our homes.

Gestapo

Our closed doors
and high walls
don't stop them.
They enter without permission,
rummaging around,
upending books—
until the words
disappear from the pages.
They play our albums too loud
and sing over the music.
They toss our cat
into the street from our balcony
and threaten our friends
over the phone.
They draw straight paths
for us to walk
and use computers
to program our poems and stories.
Our houses and schools
are hung with
blessings and good wishes
that flatter them.
They control everything
except our dreams—
and their books instruct us
that our dreams are nightmares.
They fear one day
all this will change.
We hope this fear destroys them.

Jail

You lay your head on
bent steel bars
to dream.
Your lips brush
rough walls
in song.
You sing
but even your shoes can't hear you.
You dream
but your dreams
have forgotten the way to your house.
Upon your death,
wherever it finds you,
there is no moment of silence.
No calendar marks
the occasion of your birth
as a common holiday.
Not even a tree
remembers your name.
Maybe you are even forgotten
by the ant for whose sake
you sprinkled
your ration of sugar
onto the floor.

Light and Heavy Things

A single bullet
doesn't weigh much.
It flies from a boy's gun,
where he stands on a street corner,
into an arm hanging out the window
of a distant apartment.
The bullet loses all its weight,
all its power
after tearing a hole in the arm.
It can't go any farther.
It rests.

A single bullet at rest in the victim's arm
causes pain. Another two or three
would cause more. But the arm doesn't regard this.
The victim moans. He doesn't think
more bullets would have killed him.
He doesn't think, begins to weep—
tears lighter than bullets
fall onto bed sheets
and pillows stuffed with feathers.
With a bullet at rest in his arm
the victim doesn't think
that if his nearly weightless tears
fall on the boy's heavy gun
instead of pillows and bed sheets
one day the gun would rust,
or the boy's heart would go soft as wax.

Light things take the place of heavy things;
there is nothing
to take the place of light things.

We, Every Day

Every day we
should buy flowers
or candles
or bottles for water
or plastic knives and forks –
anything can have a use in war.
We shouldn't buy toys,
shouldn't leaf through books.
We should hoard sunglasses
and umbrellas and lighters.
We should always keep biscuits
and a box of matches in our pocket
to give to someone, or to set something on fire.
We need a handkerchief, too,
for bleeding hands or burning eyes.
When the mail is delivered again,
every day a postcard
with news that we're alive
will reach our friends.
Maybe they will come here
to search for us
where people who are always searching
are lost.

People

Some people were killed while running away
and some while walking.

Those going to work started towards home instead;
those going home
arrived at the graveyard.

People hiding inside their houses were also killed,
and those, too, who were closing their front doors.

People asleep on rooftops died,
and so did people peeking out windows.

Death roamed every street
and every wall
was stained with its handprints.

The people who wet their rags
to clean the walls—
those were the last to die.

Malika/Queen

After she retires,
Malika will design canvas shoes
and gowns for poor women
on her computer,
or perhaps
open a school
and never charge the whole fee
to children
who have been through
the burning drum.
Malika will sell all her houses, cars,
and pointy brooch at half price.
Malika will breed rabbits
and clap with joy
to see their eyes sparkle at night.

Four Walls

You could call where we live
a house.
A room, very high up
with a very low ceiling,
one window, quite large,
and one very small door
that you could pass through
with your hands folded over your breast,
never lifting your feet from the floor.
You can look out this window, too,
out the window in the very high room
with the very low ceiling
if you like;
you can sleep without stretching your legs;
you can live never lifting your head.

One Day

Always in the city,
on our way from here to there,
we are afraid.
Out of nowhere
a stray bullet
might murder us.
Those of us hit by bullets
die, or, wounded,
await our turn in the hospital.
Always, news of death.
Always, heaps of burned cars—
newspapers
like firecrackers
all day
explode in our hands.
Watching our dying depart,
we don't weep anymore.
Instead of pain,
glut with smoke.
What is trampled
under foot when crowds
flee the gunfire from speeding cars?
We do not heed this.
Even after hearing
the screams of women,
rushing to take refuge in the shops,
we do not run to help.
We cross the street
as soon as we see
police and armored cars approaching.

When we hear the sirens
of ambulances and fire trucks,
no sound escapes our throats.
Through clenched teeth,
we force down sleeping pills
and put our heads on pillows
to go to sleep
and prepare for another day like this.

East

When the sun
sets to the west
we try to stop it
to hold a little bit of light.

Before evening
we go and stand by the shore
and wait for the sun.
It arrives slowly
and, never touching us,
drowns in the sea.

We return home
and go to sleep, ignoring those
who claim the sun
always rises from the east;
for them,
it cannot stop
setting in the west,
even for a day.

The Second Sky

On the first day, the clouds were wounded.
On the second day, the stars.
On the third day,
bullets struck the blue sky
and turned it black.

Something resembling tears
fell to the ground.
Sometimes the drops fell silently.
Sometimes loudly on the road: steady falling water.

The wounded sky
cried loudly.
It hid its face
in the clouds.

When we tried to lift its spirits,
the rain came faster.

Dark mud stuck to our shoes
when we came home.
The carpet
drank the sky's tears
that we spread through the house
with our damp clothes.

Our muddy footprints on the cement floor,
sometimes light, sometimes dark,
like the wounded sky.

Prayers aimed at the sky
came back with the fast rain,
and the wet earth swallowed them.

Small umbrellas were
not enough for us or the sky.
If the guns had stopped firing
in this weather,
maybe the sky would have mended
like us.

Wall and Bird

The bird dreams
it has broken
down the wall.

The bird awakens
and begins breaking down the wall
from morning to night,
keeps breaking it down
from night to morning.

One morning the wall notices
the bird has broken down.

A Child's Bicycle

A child's bicycle
is useless
on a battlefield.
It can't move
when a tank approaches,
its bells don't ring,
it seizes up,
so tiny
the tank doesn't see it.
When the tank
goes about its business,
runs over it,
a small noise
carries everywhere.
A small stain
spreads over the ground.
When the tank advances,
bicycles swarm it,
drive it crazy,
ringing their bells,
don't let it escape,
frighten it into the ether.

An Olive Tree

(For Mahmoud Darwish)

Dear friend, I have
no garden,
just a scrap from a dream, a window ledge
with a few pots
to remind me why there are trees in the world
and to tell me the trees are burning.
My sister tries to revive
my weary feet with oil.
She says what mother would tell me
if she were here —
Would that the whole world
were a well of olive oil
to revive our weary feet
so that we might walk
with those dear to us
in the gardens of paradise.
One tree will be there for you,
my friend,
forever intertwining the blessings
of healing and love.

You Are an Inflammatory Poet

Like the tear gas shells
exploding in the streets
at the protest rally
while people run this way and that,
your poems
burn the eyes,
parch the throat,
they make water pour from the nose,
and make the heart pound.
In your new poems,
instead of vines growing over
sewer pipes,
you talk instead of the dirty water.
Instead of flowers blossoming
beside the railway line
masked bandits firing guns on the express trains
is the signal of danger.
And Sindhi Hindu women's uprising
was quite upsetting.
We were celebrating the World Cup win,
firing shots in the air.
Those women were killed
purely by accident.
You should not elevate their memory in verse.
Like the opposition leader,
you disagree with our policies.
For you, all our legislation is unconstitutional,
and you refuse every bargain we offer.
Everything we do angers you.
And as for us… let's not speak of that.
Every word in your new poems

is like a bullet from a hired assassin's gun.
We could sentence you as a terrorist,
or have you declared a spy.
You could be called a traitor.
But to us, you are an inflammatory poet,
for now.

Acknowledgments

Grateful acknowledgment is made to the editors of the journals in which the following poems appeared, some in different versions:

The Annual of Urdu Studies: "Birds," "Knife," "I Will Send a Bird," "The Second Sky," the three poems titled "Poem," "Sun Stroke," "Poetry," "Time Bomb," "To Forget," "The Unworthy," "A Poem for You," "Black Bird," "My Uncle's House," "What Does Suu Kyi Want?," "Gestapo," "Jail," "We, Every Day," "People," "Light and Heavy Things";
Corresponding Voices: "Malika/Queen," "Love";
Salt Hill: "East," "A Child's Bicycle," "Wall and Bird."

Part of the Foreword to this book first appeared in *Salt Hill*.

Faisal Siddiqui: I would like to thank Raza Ali Hasan for bringing this project to me and for his continued support and mentorship. I would also like to thank Lucy Alford for her friendship, love and care and for bringing new insights into the art of poetry every day.

Christopher Kennedy and Mi Ditmar: We would like to thank Raza Ali Hasan for introducing us to Zeeshan Sahil's poems and for all of his help in the completion of this manuscript. We would also like to express our thanks and appreciation to Zeeshan's brother, Abid Raza Syed, and his sister, Afroza Khizer, for their assistance as well. And finally, we would like to thank Yasmeen Hameed for her contributions to the Foreword.

The three of us would like to thank Peter Conners and the Lannan Foundation for giving us the opportunity to publish this book, as well as Melissa Hall, Jenna Fuller, Richard Foerster, Daphne Morrissey, and Jay Muhlin for their contributions.

About the Author

Zeeshan Sahil was born on December 15, 1961 in Hyderabad, Sindh, and went to school there. He began to write poetry in 1977. He is one of the main poets who started writing prose poetry in Pakistan. During his lifetime he published eight collections of poetry in Urdu: *Arena* (1985), *Chirion ka Shor* (1989), *Kuhr Alood Aasmaan kay Sitaaray* (1994), *Karachi aur Doosri Nazmein* (1995), *Email aur Doosri Nazmein* (2003), *Shabnama aur Doosri Nazmein* (2003), *Jang ke Dinon Mein* (2003) and *Neem-tareek Muhabbat* (2005). All eight books have been published in a single volume, titled *Saari Nazmain*, and his ghazals were collected in another volume, *Wajh-e Begangi*, in 2011. One more volume of his work, containing all his uncollected and still unpublished poems is being compiled. He died on April 12, 2008 in Karachi.

About the Translators

Born and raised in Karachi, Pakistan, **Faisal Siddiqui** is a Director of services, working for a mid-size IT consulting company in Southern California. He has a BA in computer science from the University of Texas at Austin. His poems have been published in *Barrow Street, Harpur Palate, Poet Lore, Salamander, Malahat Review, New Letters, Tuesday: An Art Project* and *Notre Dame Review*.

Christopher Kennedy is the author of *Ennui Prophet* (BOA Editions, Ltd.), *Encouragement for a Man Falling to His Death* (BOA Editions, Ltd.), which received the Isabella Gardner Poetry Award in 2007, *Trouble with the Machine* (Low Fidelity Press), and *Nietzsche's Horse* (Mitki/Mitki Press). His work has appeared in many print and online journals and magazines, including *New York Tyrant, Ninth Letter, 5-Trope, The Threepenny Review, Slope, Mississippi Review, Ploughshares,* and *McSweeney's*. In 2011, he was awarded an NEA Fellowship for Poetry. A founding editor of the literary journal *3rd Bed*, he is an associate professor of English at Syracuse University where he directs the MFA Program in Creative Writing.

Mi Ditmar is the Grants Program Coordinator for The Humanities Center at Syracuse University. She received her MFA in Creative Writing at Syracuse University where she received the Joyce Carol Oates Award and the Delmore Schwartz Prize. Her poetry has appeared in *Stone Canoe* and her fiction has appeared in *The Alaska Quarterly Review* and *Prairie Schooner*.

The Lannan Translations Selection Series

Ljuba Merlina Bortolani, *The Siege*
Olga Orozco, *Engravings Torn from Insomnia*
Gérard Martin, *The Hiddenness of the World*
Fadhil Al-Azzawi, *Miracle Maker*
Sándor Csoóri, *Before and After the Fall: New Poems*
Francisca Aguirre, *Ithaca*
Jean-Michel Maulpoix, *A Matter of Blue*
Willow, Wine, Mirror, Moon: Women's Poems from Tang China
Felipe Benítez Reyes, *Probable Lives*
Ko Un, *Flowers of a Moment*
Paulo Henriques Britto, *The Clean Shirt of It*
Moikom Zeqo, *I Don't Believe in Ghosts*
Adonis (Ali Ahmad Saʿid), *Mihyar of Damascus, His Songs*
Maya Bejerano, *The Hymns of Job and Other Poems*
Novica Tadić, *Dark Things*
Praises & Offenses: Three Women Poets of the Dominican Republic
Ece Temelkuran, *Book of the Edge*
Aleš Šteger, *The Book of Things*
Nikola Madzirov, *Remnants of Another Age*
Carsten René Nielsen, *House Inspections*
Jacek Gutorow, *The Folding Star and Other Poems*
Marosa di Giorgio, *Diadem*
Zeeshan Sahil, *Light and Heavy Things*

For more on the Lannan Translations Selection Series
visit our website:
www.boaeditions.org